# I want to be a Dentist

**Other titles in this series:**

I Want to be a Builder
I Want to be a Chef
I Want to be a Cowboy
I Want to be a Doctor
I Want to be a Farmer
I Want to be a Firefighter
I Want to be a Librarian
I Want to be a Mechanic
I Want to be a Musician
I Want to be a Nurse
I Want to be a Pilot
I Want to be President
I Want to be a Police Officer
I Want to be a Scientist
I Want to be a Soldier
I Want to be a Teacher
I Want to be a Truck Driver
I Want to be a Vet
I Want to be a Zookeeper

# I WANT TO BE A
# Dentist

**DAN LIEBMAN**

FIREFLY BOOKS

# A Firefly Book

Published by Firefly Books Ltd. 2016

Copyright © 2016 Firefly Books Ltd.

First Printing

**Publisher Cataloging-in-Publication Data (U.S.)**

Names: Liebman, Daniel, author.
Title: I want to be a dentist / Dan Liebman.
Description: Richmond Hill, Ontario, Canada : Firefly Books, 2016. | Series: I want to be a-- | Summary: "A picture book for children who want to know how to become a dentist, what a dentist does, and what makes it fun" — Provided by publisher.
Identifiers: ISBN 978-1-77085-786-5 (hardcover) | 978-1-77085-785-8 (paperback)
Subjects: LCSH: Dentists — Juvenile literature. | Dentists – Vocational guidance – Juvenile literature.
Classification: LCC RK63.L543 |DDC 617.6 – dc23

Published in the United States by
Firefly Books (U.S.) Inc.
P.O. Box 1338, Ellicott Station
Buffalo, New York 14205

Published in Canada by
Firefly Books Ltd.
50 Staples Avenue, Unit 1
Richmond Hill, Ontario L4B 0A7

**Library and Archives Canada Cataloguing in Publication**

Liebman, Daniel, author
I want to be a dentist / Dan Liebman.

(I want to be a)
ISBN 978-1-77085-785-8 (paperback).—ISBN 978-1-77085-786-5 (hardcover)

1. Dentistry—Juvenile literature. I. Title.

RK63.L53 2016                 j617.6
C2016-901035-X

**Photo Credits:**

© wavebreakmedia/shutterstock: page 18, cover

© schegi/shutterstock: page 20

© Parisa Michailidis: pages 5, 12, 23

© Cathy Hoshino: pages 11, 17

© Mat Hayward/shutterstock: page 21

© George Walker: pages 6,7, 8–9, 10, 13, 14–15, 16, 19, 22, 24, back cover

Special thanks are extended to the following dentists and their staffs: Dr. Joshua Charlat, Dr. Tony Mitilineos, Dr. M. Shorser and Dr. Nibu Varguise.

Printed in China

*The Publisher acknowledges the financial support for our publishing program by the Government of Canada through the Canada Book Fund as administered by the Department of Canadian Heritage.*

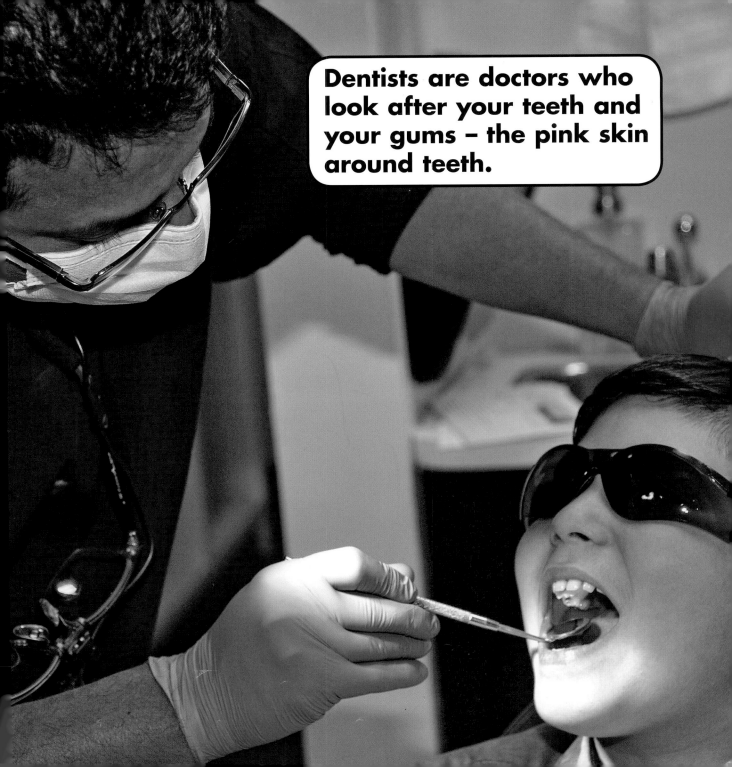

The receptionist is in charge of the dentist's appointments.

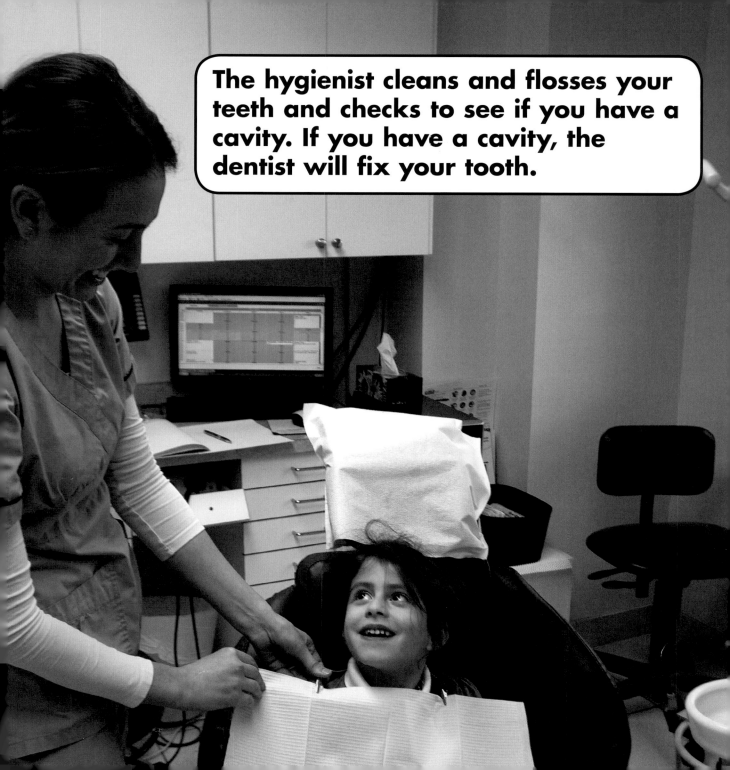

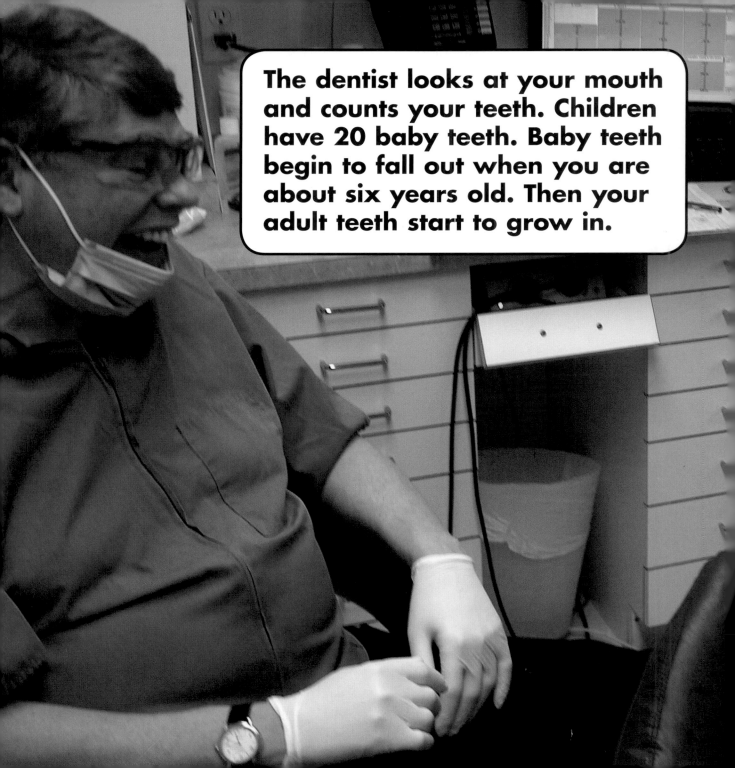

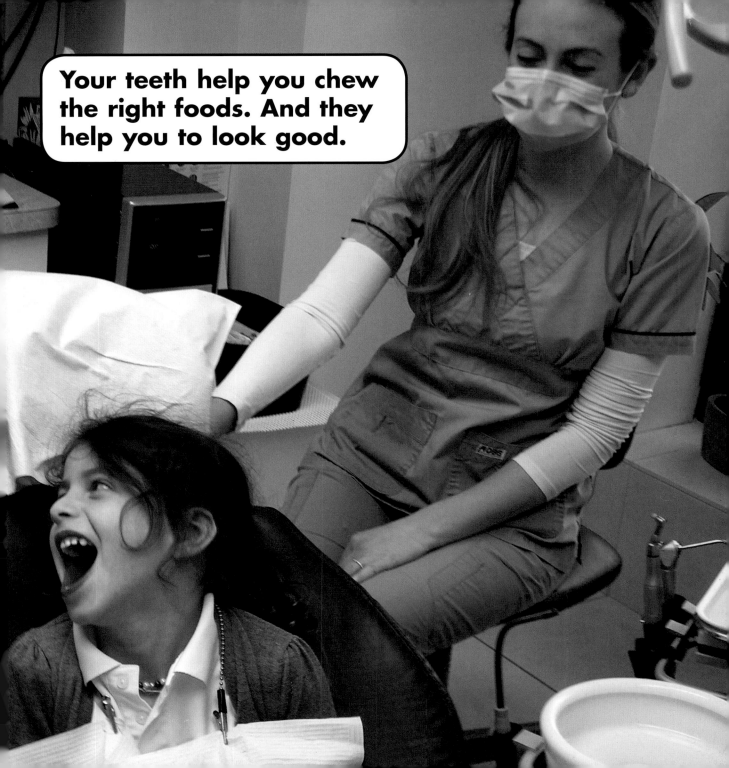

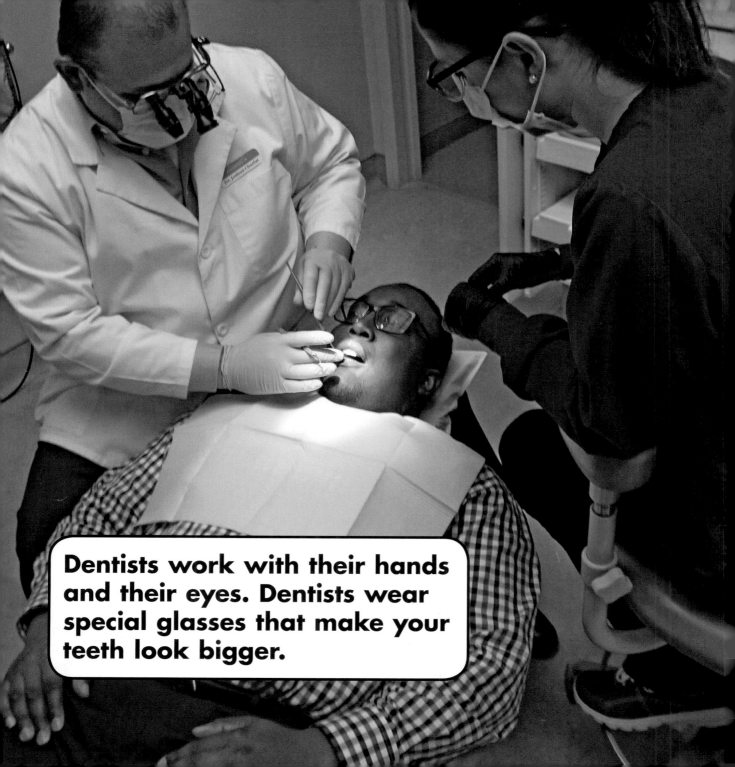

Dentists work with their hands and their eyes. Dentists wear special glasses that make your teeth look bigger.

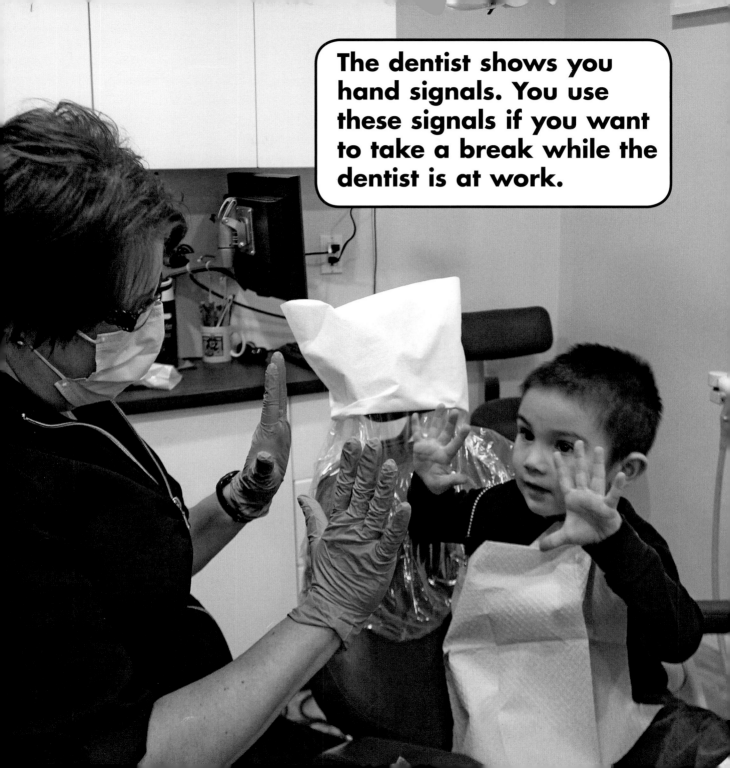

Dentists use small tools, such as this tiny mirror. This boy is wearing special glasses because the dentist uses a bright light.

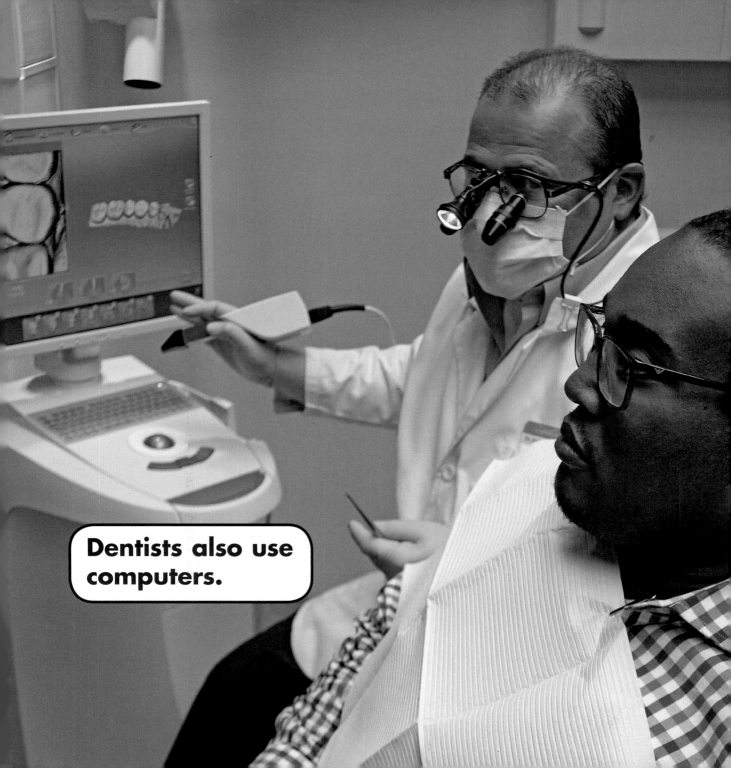

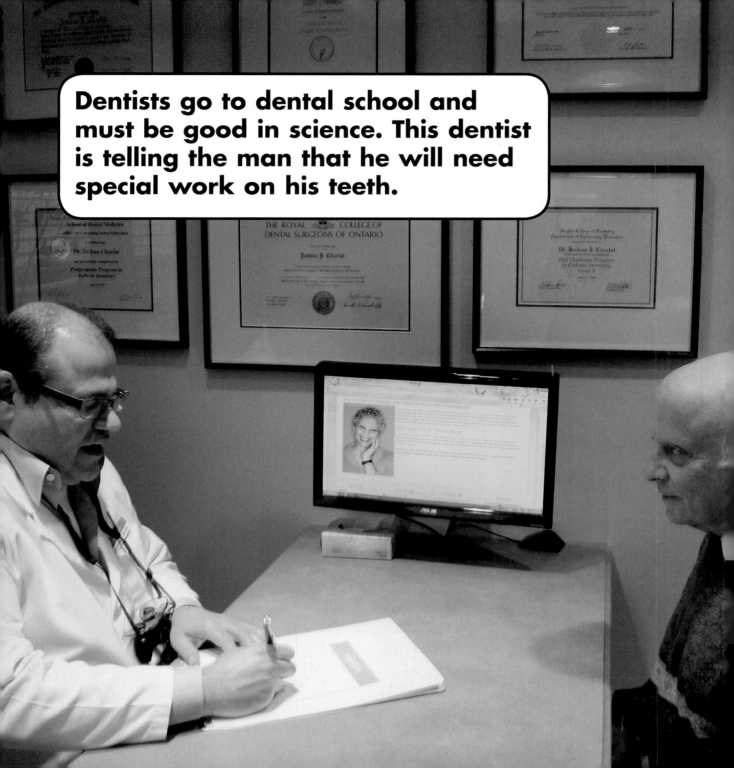

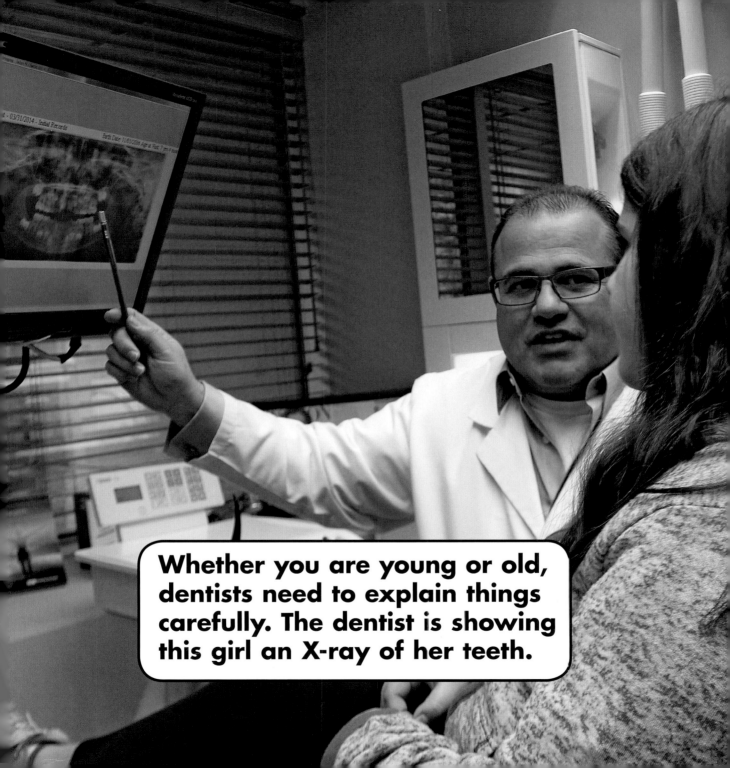

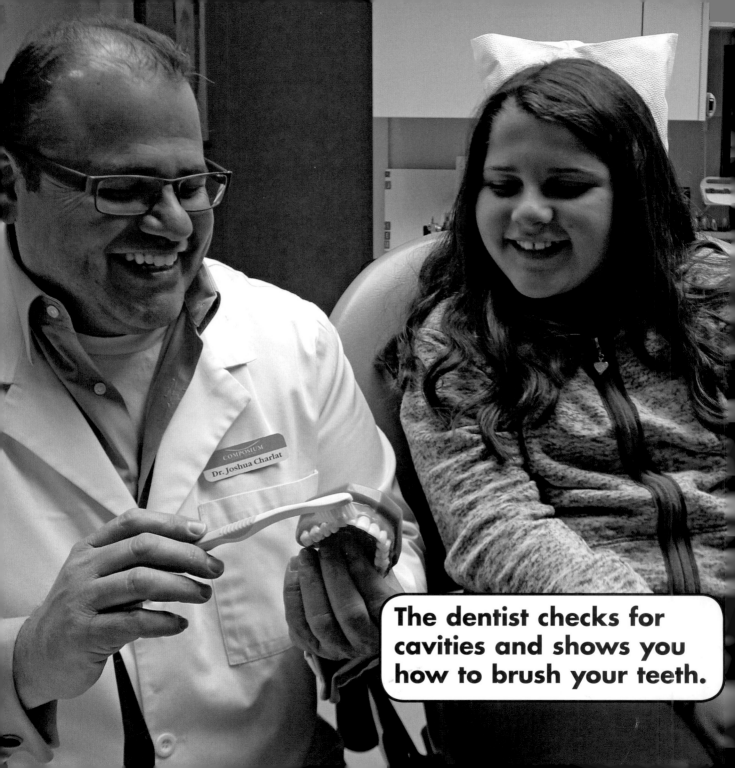

The dentist checks for cavities and shows you how to brush your teeth.

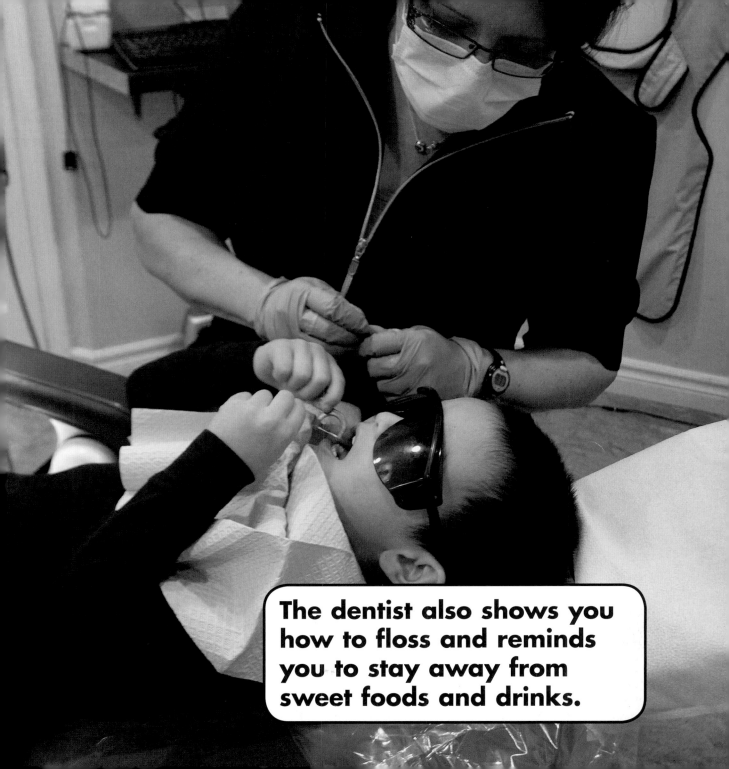

The dentist also shows you how to floss and reminds you to stay away from sweet foods and drinks.

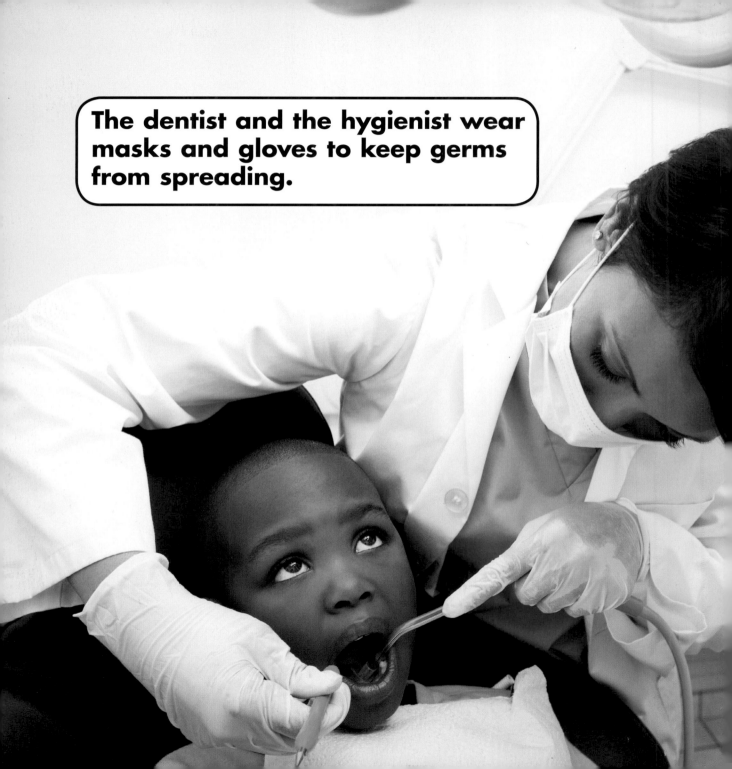

The dentist and the hygienist wear masks and gloves to keep germs from spreading.

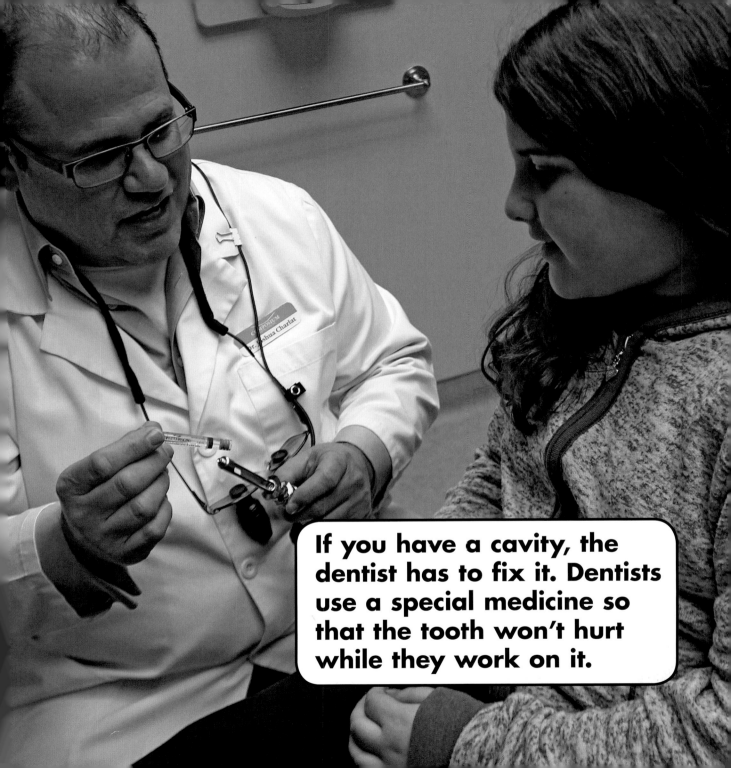

If you have a cavity, the dentist has to fix it. Dentists use a special medicine so that the tooth won't hurt while they work on it.

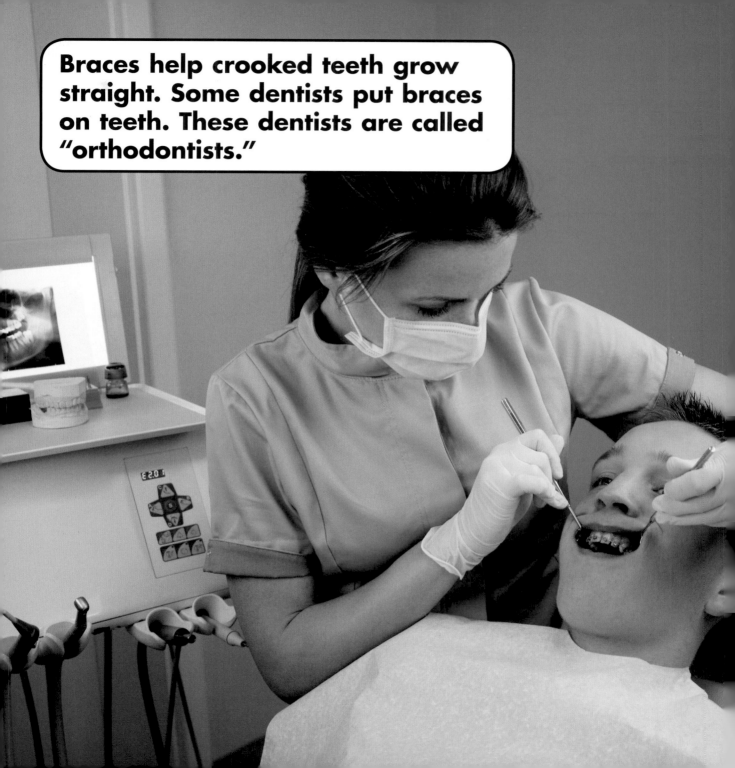

When you leave the office, the dentist gives you a new toothbrush. And sometimes you even get a present!